Leadership

People Leave A Bad Boss More Than They Leave A Bad Job Inspire And Exert Some Control Over Your Workforce

(The Most Powerful Strategies To Help You Become A Better Leader)

Florentino Spence

TABLE OF CONTENT

Introduction 1

Enhancing Your Capabilities In The Area Of Communication In Order To Become A More Effective Leader 7

The Leader Of The Organized Group 22

Be Aware Of What Is Happening In Your Environment 27

Comprehending The Meaning Of Leadership . 38

Theories Regarding Leadership 42

Comprehending The Members Of Generation Y And The Characteristics That Define Them 47

Always Aim Before You Jump. 69

Accountability As Well As Availability For Contact 74

Increasing One's Self-Assurance While At Work 83

A Formula For Quicker Results As A Framework 94

Setting A Course Of Action And A Vision Are Both Essential Components Of Effective Leadership 111

The Demonstration Of Leadership Requires Consistency. 119

Diversity And Equal Opportunity For Everyone 149

There Are A Lot Of Surprising Facts About Angela Merkel That You Probably Don't Know. 159

The Art Of Influencing Others 166

Several Useful Pointers Regarding The Search For Inspiration.. 171

Conventions Governing Businesses Often Require Participation In Negotiations 179

General Approaches To The Evaluation Of Individuals... 183

Introduction

We would like to take this opportunity to welcome you to Leadership: Influential Leadership Skills for Mastering Business Communication, Management Conversations, and Team Building. This all-encompassing book eliminates the fluff in order to give useful knowledge that you can begin putting to use right away. For example, rather than spending page after page discussing the chemical processes that take place inside our brains when we speak, or using jargon that is decades old and taken from outdated textbooks, the authors of this book cut out the filler. Each page has pertinent material that is ready to be used, and the reader is actively urged to contribute to the knowledge that is provided and make use of it to establish their own particular methods and style. The book was written to be read from beginning to end; but, if a certain chapter is of special interest to you, please feel free to hop forward to it. For example, if you are interested in getting a pay raise today, you may want to skip ahead to the section titled "Influential Phrases."

Each part provides an in-depth examination of a distinct subject. They are ordered in such a way as to build upon each other as they go towards the final chapter, which will explain how to put everything together as well as which forms of leadership and ways of communication are most effective in a given circumstance.

You will have a better understanding of what your superiors and team members expect from you as a leader as a result of the high-level content that is presented throughout this book. You will also learn how to manage and direct these expectations so that they consistently lead to favorable results. This book contains a variety of models, strategies, and tactics that cover a wide range of themes and issues. These models, strategies, and tactics may be used alone or in combination to express your views and direct interactions with any number of different individuals in any given circumstance. This book is primarily framed within the context of the workplace; however, whether you are a football coach, sales manager, financial advisor, or entrepreneur, this book has information relevant to your day-to-day business interactions, and when utilized appropriately, it will significantly improve both your output and your ability to advance within your chosen field.

This book is centered on your experiences and should be combined with the information that you currently possess in order to achieve the goal of having a stronger impact within both your workplace and the industry as a whole. If you go through the exercises and use the models provided for making decisions, you will discover that you have increased confidence in both your ability to manage and to delegate tasks.

Understand and discover how to coach people to achieve their best achievements via the use of Systematic Thinking, comprehension, and feedback, while simultaneously boosting the functioning and productivity of any team using the proven outcome management strategies outlined inside Managing Outcomes.

The chapters "Influential Phrases You can use Today" and "Quick Fire Tactics You can use Today" were written with the intention of providing, at a glance, helpful advice and strategies on the most efficient methods to ask inquiries, make requests, and delegate tasks.

Your crew is the most valuable resource at your disposal. Their one-of-a-kind set of abilities and beliefs will contribute to the results of the group in ways that will often seem to be random. But if you work on developing both yourself and your team, you will start to see patterns within the system, have a better sense of what will happen next, and be aware of the appropriate communication and management styles to apply in order to effectively influence the situation in the direction of the end you want. Do not allow yourself to be controlled by your environment; instead, cultivate, improve, and perfect your abilities to communicate, exert influence, and make decisions in order to become the most powerful leader you possibly can.

Enhancing Your Capabilities In The Area Of Communication In Order To Become A More Effective Leader

We often find ourselves in positions of leadership in a variety of settings and contexts. This includes leadership at the family level, as well as leadership at the organizational level and the national level. The desire to be a better leader comes easily to anybody who finds themselves in a position of authority, regardless of the level at which they find themselves. Despite this, there aren't too many people who have managed to be successful in this area. The inability of leaders to effectively communicate with their followers is one of the crucial instruments that brings down the effectiveness of leadership.

The exchange of information between individuals is accomplished via the process of communication. It was either expressive or receptive at the same time.

The growth of both your professional and personal life depends heavily on your ability to communicate clearly and fluently. It is also essential to the process of achieving greatness in leadership. Therefore, everyone who aspires to achieve leadership excellence should make it a priority to cultivate a mindset that prioritizes clear and effective communication, and they should make it a point to consistently improve on the art of leadership communication even before they achieve any degree of leadership position. By properly motivating and inspiring their people, good leaders are able to effectively communicate with them. In addition, the most successful businesses make communication both clear and efficient in order to foster a culture of discipline, responsibility, and strategic alignment.

Communication is Comprised of Three Elements: the Verbal Message (the Words We Choose), the Para-Verbal Messages (How We Say the Words), and the Nonverbal Messages (Our Body Language). Messages that are lucid and to the point may be sent with the help of these three components. In addition to this, we rely on them to successfully receive and interpret the signals that are given to us. It is common for there to be confusion when the verbal component, for example, states "yes," while the nonverbal component reveals "no." In order to communicate well, one has to coordinate the three components of communication such that they accurately depict the message that is being conveyed.

Listening is the process of acquiring the information that has been delivered. Listening is an essential part of the communication process that takes one's full attention and effort. It requires developing a psychological connection with the person doing the talking. It also requires a willingness to try to see things from the speaker's point of view and a desire to do so. At this stage in the conversation, it is imperative that the listener refrain from passing judgment or making an appraisal of the message, and instead retain an open mind about it. Listening nonverbally is providing the speaker with one's entire physical attention or being aware of the speaker's nonverbal signals, while listening verbally entails paying attention to the words that are being spoken as well as the emotions that are being communicated. Verbal, nonverbal, and para-verbal listening are all important components of effective feedback collection for leaders, just as they are when passing on information to their followers.

Effective communicators convey their messages by taking into account the following considerations at the proper times:

1. The readability of the message (i.e., make it straightforward and easy to understand).

2. The adequacy of the communication, defined as the provision of sufficient data for accurate comprehension

3. The reliability of the communication (ensuring that it is as accurate as the initial information).

4. The timing of the message (having it delivered at the right time and in the right location).

It is necessary for the communicator to ask for or solicit feedback from the listener to ensure that the message is being received and comprehended in order for there to be successful communication. In a nutshell, someone who is skilled in communication should also be skilled in the art of listening.

Additional helpful hints for strong communication skills are as follows:

1. Make sure you're making eye contact with the others in the room.

2. Have body awareness and project an air of self-assurance and persuasion.

3. Facial expressions and gestural patterns.

4. Express one's own opinions and ideas.

5. Get in the habit of using your communication abilities effectively.

The process of effective communication involves participation from both parties. It entails transmitting the message while simultaneously soliciting response (active listening). It represents both the speaker's and the listener's culpability in the situation. It is quite easy to understand, and there is no tension present.

Making It Occur Through Efficient and Successful Execution

Developing objectives, making plans, and making arrangements are topics that we have previously covered. Everything is documented and firmly established in stone. It is time to start putting your strategy into action at this point.

Without putting these plans and aspirations into action, none of them will amount to anything.

They will never be finished since no action was ever done to move them forward. That's like planting a seed but never giving it the water, sunshine, or food it needs to grow into a full-grown plant.

In this chapter, you will learn how to create basic execution skills, which will make it second nature for you to take on any problem. Let's get started and transform you into a leader who is ready to act as soon as the word 'go' is said.

Get rid of your worries and ideas that are holding you back.

It's possible that your insecurities and self-limiting ideas are one of the things holding you back. There is going to be worry about "what if it isn't good enough" or "what if this fails," both of which are reasonable worries. You, on the other hand, have the capacity to triumph over your fears and limiting beliefs with time and effort.

After you have succeeded in overcoming these challenges, it will be much simpler for you to take action. You will have unwavering confidence in your capacity to do whatever it is you set out to do. And a change will occur in your attitude, leading you to re-identify failure as a setback.

You have already developed a strategy to use in the event that you face a challenge. It is possible for you to finish it with little to no hesitance. When a genuine leader is knocked from their horse, they quickly get back up and continue leading.

Try new things without being frightened of failing. Leaders do not always choose the path of least resistance. They are willing to take chances because they are aware of the fact that their success is entirely up to them.

Have a conversation with your team about your intentions and ambitions.

Even if your objectives and strategies are already mapped out, you and your team should still discuss them. Discuss what has to be done, what difficulties will be encountered (and how to overcome them), and other related topics. Have a discussion about the actions that each member of your team is required to perform (as well as the resources that they need to complete the task).

Inquire as to whether or if they have any queries. Give them the opportunity to voice their concerns and engage in a conversation about potential solutions. In the event that a problem is found, plans and objectives may be revised prior to their implementation. It is infinitely better to take action and then watch something bad happen rather than take preventative measures.

When everyone is on the same page as you, then it is time to act. Stop putting it off any longer and get it done.

Bring your objectives into focus.

You need to make sure that the expectations you establish are crystal clear and easy to comprehend before you proceed. What specific information about what has to be done does each member of your team need to be aware of? What exactly does it mean to be successful, and what does it mean to be unsuccessful?

Develop some habits.

If you want the execution to go more smoothly than was indicated, you are going to need to create some routines. What exactly are the activities that need to be finished? What is the methodical, step-by-step approach?

Show the other members of your team what they need to do in order to accomplish the work with the least amount of effort possible. The only thing that will be required of them is to place an order for a cup of coffee. It is essential that you be ready to make modifications in the event that circumstances arise that are beyond of everyone's control (and that you communicate these adjustments to your team).

Keep track of and assess all advancements.

Earlier in this tutorial, we touched on the importance of keeping track of your progress. This involves keeping a record of, and conducting an analysis of, the metrics that are essential to the accomplishment of your goals. When you go through the progress that has been made each week, be sure to take notes on what is and is not working.

It's possible that you've noticed that your daily or weekly goals aren't being met. What may possibly be the issue? It's possible that you'll need to seek for trends and make adjustments as necessary.

It's conceivable that one of the people in your team is having trouble with something. As a consequence of this, it could be a good idea to have a conversation with them and find out what's going on.

Delegate power to the members of your team.

If you give your team members the authority to work together and encourage them to do so, they will be able to do so effectively. If you do not do this, it will lead to them being dissatisfied, unproductive, and not in the correct frame of mind to achieve the objectives that you have set for them.

We will circle back around to this subject at a later point in the course. Having said that, it is of the utmost importance to make it so that every single person of your team feels that they are a significant component of something really amazing.

A Few Parting Thoughts

The ability to effectively execute plans is what ultimately leads to the accomplishment of objectives. If your worries and self-limiting ideas come in the way, you won't be able to follow through. Once you have eliminated their obstruction, there is nothing that can stop you.

Ensure that the members of your team fully understand your plans, objectives, and expectations. Establish routines in such a way that their achievements seem virtually simple to complete. Keeping track of progress naturally opens up new doors for further action based on the accomplishments and objectives that have been established.

The Leader Of The Organized Group

To be organized, you need to think in a way that is systematic and effective. You are also need to have an understanding of the various, cohesive elements that make up a whole as well as the unique roles that each portion serves. An organized leader is someone who recognizes the need of striking this delicate balance and is able to make strategic work assignments to the appropriate team members in order to maintain it.

Being well-organized is a skill that can be used to almost any effort successfully. Because they are aware of the who, how, where, and why of the situation, leaders who possess this quality are able to keep their minds clear throughout the whole of the process of carrying out a project.

The organized leader is aware of both his or her own capabilities and those of the other members of the team, including both their strengths and their limitations. This leader is able to delegate each assignment to the appropriate department in spite of the growing volume of work that has to be done. This methodical approach will guarantee that both the performance and the product are of a high quality.

The Process of Becoming One:

Having an ordered approach to life is essential to realizing any goal you set for yourself in this world. Leaders should have the ability to properly organize and allocate work in order for the group to achieve their shared objective. You may become a more organized leader by putting these methods into practice:

Honor the variety of cultures. Recognize that each member of the team has both capabilities that will assist the team as a whole and deficiencies that may be compensated for by the strengths of other members of the team. Pay close attention to what each individual can contribute to the team, and have faith that they will be able to operate at their highest potential.

Create an unmistakable code of conduct. It is crucial for a leader to make certain that everyone completely knows their position, as well as what is expected of them. Everyone in the group, especially the person in charge, has to understand the significance of their own role in comparison to the roles of the other members. When this is made perfectly obvious to everyone, the rules of the team will start to make a great deal of sense to everyone, which means that everyone will be more inclined to adhere to them.

Give credit to those who deserve it. Recognizing and appreciating the unique contributions of each team member is one of the duties that falls on the shoulders of the leader of an organization. It is true that you all collaborate on projects, but it does not imply that each individual does not possess a mind that is capable of independent thought. Each individual still has an insatiable need for validation for their efforts, particularly from the person in charge of the group. You are encouraging that member to continue to put in their best effort by granting this request.

Ensure that the surrounding area is kept orderly. It goes without saying that in order to be an effective leader of an organized group, you need to walk the walk. Keeping a tidy and well-organized workstation is the quickest and easiest approach to demonstrate this quality to others. Because you no longer have to rummage through piles of documents in search of a single document, you are able to work more quickly and effectively in such an environment. At the end of each day, you should make sure that your area is tidy and that everything is placed back where it belongs.

Instead of trying to become better at being organized, you should focus on adopting a minimalist lifestyle. Eliminate any stuff (and people) that just serve to clutter your environment and thinking by getting rid of them. This will allow only the most important things to shine out. By coming up with a straightforward plan of action, everything will become more straightforward and simpler to handle.

Be Aware Of What Is Happening In Your Environment.

The last thing that a good leader should bear in mind is how essential it is to have a deep comprehension of the culture that they are a part of. You need to have an understanding of the kinds of things that the people around you desire, as well as the reasons why a certain product or service succeeds in a particular culture but fails to succeed in others.

People's means of making decisions, the way they talk and interact with one another, the tales they tell their children and grandchildren, the myths and legends that are passed down, and the methods of doing labor are all fundamental components of culture. It is also about the customs and mannerisms of a certain location or nation; however, in this case, we are speaking about the culture of your job.

It is also believed that culture is something that can be learnt and that it reveals a great deal about the manner in which the people who live in a certain location behave. What really essential is that you educate yourself on the culture of the location you are in so that you are aware of what you can contribute and so that you can learn more about the people who are in your immediate environment.

How exactly are you supposed to comprehend, or at the very least obtain a feel for, what is occurring in the workplace? You may easily do the following by doing so:

Take Stock of Your Circumstances

Do a quick scan of your environment. You are able to accomplish this goal by asking certain sorts of questions, such as those that will assist you in gaining a better understanding of the situation at hand and in determining what actions you may take next. The following are some examples of possible questions:

Where exactly are all of the many departments that make up your office located?

What kinds of things do individuals keep on their workstations?

What are some common topics of conversation during breaks?

What do individuals talk about in their e-mails and letters to one another?

How often do individuals use their phones, other electronic devices, and computers?

How would you characterize the tenor of your messages? How do you communicate with other people? Do you present a welcoming demeanor or do you intimidate them?

What kinds of movies and television programs do they like watching? Which songs are now enjoying a lot of success?

What kind of garments do they put on their bodies?

What can you notice hanging on the walls or posted on the bulletin boards?

What kinds of foods do individuals like eating?

What kinds of things do individuals do in the various regions of your office?

What kind of reactions do people have toward you and toward one another?

What exactly are the contents of your memos?

In addition to that, remember to be observant!

Take a look at the activities going on in the area around you. Check out what others have displayed on their workstations or walls, observe what they are wearing, and make an effort to learn what it is that they enjoy to listen to or watch in their spare time. In this manner, it will be simple for you to comprehend what could be successful and what may not, and it will be simple for you to devise goods and services that will be beneficial to the individuals concerned.

Learn to see past your feelings. Because a person's core beliefs may be inferred from the feelings he experiences, it is essential to have an understanding of the circumstances that either bring them joy or cause them sorrow. You also need to figure out what kinds of things excite them and what kinds of things they could care less about.

Observe the manner in which your followers communicate with one another. You will have an understanding of what drives them or what causes them to become agitated in this manner. As you can see, the people around you are pretty much a representation of the individuals you would want to follow you or purchase your goods, and as a result, it is very crucial that you know what they want and what they do not want.

Look for hints that aren't being spoken. You read in a previous chapter about the significance of non-verbal communication; you should focus on improving this skill. You should educate yourself not only in the art of nonverbal communication for yourself, but also in the art of interpreting the nonverbal communication of others who are in your immediate environment.

If you keep these things in mind, there is a good chance that you will become the sort of leader that not only you, but also the people around you, will be proud of.

An Assessment of Performance

The performance review of employees is often a stressful affair, both for the manager and for the individual being evaluated. This is true in both cases. It is a signal to the staff that there will come a moment when they will be held accountable for all of the actions, both deliberate and careless, that they have carried out over the year. It is a period when the management is forced to do the painful task of writing down all of their actions of omission and commission that occurred during the course of the year. But there's no reason why it should be such a terrible encounter.

The following are some of the ways in which an effective manager may transform an annual event that is often dreaded into a satisfying and fruitful activity.

Keep an eye on the performance of your employees.

There are two very effective methods for measuring the performance of staff members. The first option is for the management to maintain notes on the performance of each employee, and the second option is for the employee to keep notes discussing his or her own performance throughout the year. In the eyes of the management, the shortcomings of the employee will overwhelm his triumphs, whereas in the eyes of the employee, the manager's successes will overshadow the employee's failings. This is because of the human nature. Therefore, the technique in which the employee and the management take records on the employee's performance over the year will emphasize both the employee's triumphs and failures during the course of the year.

Put an emphasis on accomplishments.

When management places more of an emphasis on an employee's triumphs rather than their failings, employee retention rates increase. When one considers the bigger picture, it is clear that the individual and collective achievements of members of an organization are what keep it going forward throughout the year. The company would come to a screeching stop if the failings of the employees were allowed to overshadow the triumphs of the company's other workers. This insight holds true for the globe in general; the reason the world continues to turn is not because of the wicked acts of a minority of the human population, but rather the good deeds of the majority of the human population. When a firm recognizes its employees' achievements, the employees feel more inspired, and their commitment to the company becomes stronger.

But does this imply that managers should not point up when employees make mistakes?

areas that may need some work.

Take the term "failure" out of your lexicon entirely when it comes to performance review. In its place, you should write "areas of improvement." First of all, the word "Failure" is more harsher than the phrase "Failure," which suggests that the employee has arrived at a point from which there is no way out. On the other hand, the phrase "Areas of improvement" gives the impression that the employee has access to a number of different opportunities to enhance his performance.

It is possible that the manager may suggest enrolling the employee in a training program, the specifics of which will be determined by the management based on the individual's areas of weakness in terms of performance. After the training has been completed, the manager is obligated to organize a feedback session with the employee in order to assess what the employee has learnt from the training and how she plans to utilize the training components in order to enhance her performance at work. Additionally, it is a good idea to organize a presentation by the employee to other workers on the training that she has received; in this manner, the advantages of the training are passed on to other employees at no additional expense to the organization.

Setting up frequent counseling sessions with the employee is another action the manager may take to assist the employee in improving his performance. These meetings should take place on a regular basis. The management is able to keep track of the employee's pace of progress and pinpoint the specific areas in which the employee struggles to carry out the duties that have been allocated to him or her thanks to these sessions.

Even after doing all of the steps outlined above, there is still a possibility that the employee may not be able to reach the levels of improvement that are needed. This is a glaring indicator that the individual does not possess the fundamental skills necessary to complete the duties of that specific profession. As a result, it could be a good idea for the manager to suggest that she be transferred to a new department of the company, one in which her skills might be put to greater use.

Comprehending The Meaning Of Leadership

What does the term "leadership" mean to you, in your own words? You would be somewhat correct in asserting that leadership entails having the ability to exercise authority over others. People follow the commands of leaders. If you argue that it's about managing people, then you are somewhat accurate about that, too. People are, in fact, managed by leaders. If you define leadership as the capacity to guide other people, then you are still correct in your assessment of the concept. People are said to be leaders due to the fact that they effectively lead other individuals. All of these definitions are correct, however some of them are missing something. Why? Because each of these definitions focuses on the person who is leading and does not take into account the other people, whether they be members of the staff or the team itself.

Being able to share your life with the people you are leading is an essential component of true leadership. When it comes to planning, a leader is not doing his job properly if he does not include his followers in the process. A leader who works everything out on their own and does not engage in teamwork is still a leader, but they are not a very good one. Strong leadership qualities are not possessed by a leader who can manage his team members but does not give them the freedom to pursue the activities that would bring them the most joy. Everyone has the potential to lead others, but not everyone has the potential to do it effectively.

There are a lot of individuals that want to take the helm. Why? mostly due to the fact that a lot of individuals want to be heard. Everyone has the desire to always be correct, to be the one others listen to, and to be the person others feel comfortable confiding in. However, the ability to lead is just one aspect of what it means to be a leader. Leadership is the capacity to develop a vision with your team, bring together individuals who share that vision with you, and then bring that vision to life. Leadership is the ability to make that vision into reality. It is not about attempting to change people's opinions or to manage the lives of others; rather, it is about demonstrating that you are doing what you preach. People who observe you putting your words into action will get the impression that you are an influential and inspirational person. Instead than simply talking about it, put your words into action. Doing so is one of the hallmarks of a successful leader.

It's a common misconception that leadership just entails having the capacity to control other people and getting them to do what you want them to, but that's not how it works at all. It is not about having the strong and authoritative stature or the abundant intellect that would garner people's respect. Rather, it is about having the ability to influence other people. It is composed of a variety of features taken together. Leadership is about possessing the traits that would allow your team stay together and accomplish a job as a unit as a cohesive whole.

You are going to learn about various attributes that a good leader must possess in order for them to be successful in the chapters that follow this one. All of these characteristics are fundamental, but they are absolutely necessary for developing your leadership abilities. Examine them to determine whether or not you have excellent leadership traits, and if you don't, discover how to develop those abilities if you still don't have them.

Theories Regarding Leadership

This article will explore two distinct groups of ideas. The first category of ideas is known as universalist theories, and they propose that there is only one method of leadership that is appropriate for use in each given circumstance. The second school of thought is known as contingency theory, and it is based on the fundamental notion that various circumstances call for unique styles of leadership in order to be successful. The theories acknowledge not just the influence of the environment, but also the role that individual characteristics have in shaping leadership behavior.

Theories held by Universalists a) The Approach Centered on Great Men

The oldest and most basic conception of leadership was that leaders are born, and that the attributes that distinguished historical personalities such as Jesus Christ, Winston Churchill, Alexander the Great, and Joan of Arc, such as a great vision, a high level of competence, and a decent personality, were inherited. According to this interpretation, the fact that influential people tend to come from the same families strengthens the case that there is a genetic basis for leadership. It was said that individuals with such characteristics are destined for positions of prominence in society.

This method has been criticized for a variety of reasons, one of which is that its adoption may lead to a legitimization of favoritism in staff advancement when relatives of previous successful executives migrate into an organization. This is one of the critiques that has been leveled against this method. In addition, if the viewpoint that "leaders are born, not made" is accepted, then companies must only hire people who were born to be leaders into their workforce. Not only is this impossible, but accepting this view will render management training programs irrelevant because the staff that is recruited will be born leaders who may not require any additional training.

b) The Approach Based on Traits and Characteristics

This method is somewhat similar to the "great man" method in several respects. For instance, it operates on the presumption that the characteristics of a successful leader are absolutely necessary for that role's fulfillment. However, it does not highlight that leaders are born with particular personality qualities, but rather that certain attributes, whether they are intrinsic or learned, are necessary for effective leadership. This is a significant difference from the other approach.

The issue with using this technique is that it might be difficult to accurately quantify a number of personal qualities. For instance, it might be difficult to determine how much intellect a person has, despite the fact that this is an important trait for effective leaders. Additionally, although physical characteristics such as "height" and "appearance" may be seen, psychological characteristics such as "perseverance," "initiative," and "intelligence" cannot. Because psychological characteristics cannot be directly seen, evidence of their existence may only be inferred from behavior, which is fraught with the risk of drawing incorrect conclusions. In addition, characteristics exhibited by effective leaders are often evaluated as having high worth (for example, decisive, intelligent, powerful, etc.), although the majority of leaders frequently display negative qualities, which are not explicitly included here.

Comprehending The Members Of Generation Y And The Characteristics That Define Them

The inability of members of Generation X and Baby Boomers to comprehend members of the Y Generation is the primary contributor to the difficulties experienced by managers of workers who are mostly members of that generation. Because baby boomers are not familiar with the qualities and features of Generation Y, they find it difficult to effectively lead this generation.

We are going to talk about Generation Y and try to have a better understanding of them in this chapter. The objective of this is to provide you with the education that will enable you to comprehend members of the generation Y and communicate effectively with them. In addition, in order for you to comprehend why there is a generation gap in the first place, we are going to focus specifically on the ways in which Millennials are distinct from both Generation X and Baby Boomers.

Exploring Further: Gaining an Understanding of the Millennial Generation

After the vast baby boomer generation, the generation known as Generation Y has become the biggest cohort to enter the workforce. As a result, it is crucial for every manager to comprehend the millennial generation. As we previously said, the majority of persons serving in management jobs in today's organizations are baby boomers.

In particular, the Millennial generation have a great deal of expertise in the area of technology, and they also have a solid educational foundation. The vast majority of Millennials have obtained an education of high quality, making them very competitive and skilled in their chosen fields.

They operate with a great deal of fire and enthusiasm, and their energy levels are over the roof. They are able to multitask with relative ease because to their heavy reliance on technology, which provides them with a variety of tools, appliances, and equipment to choose from while fulfilling their responsibilities.

The fact that Generation Y has such lofty aspirations stems directly from the high standards they've set for themselves. They do not accept mediocrity; rather, they strive for greatness in whatever they do. Their goal is to attain excellence in all they do; hence, they make use of various technical devices and cutting-edge techniques in their work in order to accomplish remarkable outcomes and get the most benefit from their efforts.

The members of Generation Y are known for their love of adventure and their enjoyment of working in environments that include healthy competition. They do not like to make forward plans, particularly if they are not the ones who are creating the plans, since they believe that everything should be earned via hard labor. They strive very hard to achieve a balance in their personal and professional life, despite the fact that they hunger for a challenging work environment and actively seek out new challenges in their workplace.

Additionally, Millennials have a strong desire to interact with their peers. They dislike being alone and get their energy from engaging with other people. Because of this, they throw a lot of parties in order to increase the number of chances they have to talk to new people. This helps explain why people prefer to operate in teams rather than alone.

Millennials are known to have a short attention span and a need for instant fulfillment as a result of their high levels of physical and mental energy. They dislike having to wait for things to happen and are unable to wait patiently for an effort to show its effects over a period of weeks or months, let alone years. They find it difficult to wait. They are often sidetracked because of their need for instant gratification, which makes it difficult for them to focus on a certain goal. Because of this, members of this generation may have difficulty in fully materializing their long-term objectives.

Millennials are a generation that values rapid progress in every endeavor or business they pursue, and as a consequence, they expect to see results immediately. Previous generations have a negative perception of this generation's thirst for swift and rapid improvements because of their own impatience.

Additionally, Millennials are very creative people that strive for innovation in all they do. Because they are often bored and impatient, they are always looking for new ways to complete tasks, which enables them to develop original thoughts and ideas because they are forced to think outside the box.

Let's talk about why there is a generation gap between the millennial generation and the generations who came before them, particularly the Baby Boomers, now that we've gone over the fundamental and essential qualities of the millennial generation.

Leadership is a way of behaving rather than a title or position.

This indicates that your actions will decide the kind of leader you will be in the future. The fact that you have been promoted does not automatically make you the most effective leader. People have been promoted simply because they had been in the same job for a long time, despite the fact that some of these individuals had the leadership abilities of a wet paper bag. I have seen this happen. You may rest easy knowing that folks who do things like this are eventually exposed. It is possible for anybody, regardless of their status or position, to take on the role of a leader. After completing their training, the majority of officers in the British army are assigned to a specific regiment. There are Soldiers, Corporals, Sergeants, and so on throughout these units that have greater experience than the Officer. The command is depending on these soldiers to take charge until the Officer has a better grasp on the situation. The same thing might happen at a firm when an individual graduates from college and immediately begins working in a management capacity. Always remember to act and behave like a leader should, regardless of what position you hold, since your role as a leader requires you to encourage and motivate the people working under your supervision.

The second most effective strategy for influencing other people's opinions is to lead by example.

In a nutshell, you should never, under any circumstances, ask another person to carry out an activity that you would not carry out yourself. For instance, if you wanted everyone to help clean up, you should first assign responsibilities to the other people, and then get started cleaning up after yourself. It is important to overcome your fear of getting your hands filthy. If you want to be a successful leader, you need to have the guts to take the initiative and do things the right way first. People will see whether you set a good or terrible example and respond accordingly, thus it is important to keep in mind that you should constantly be aware of your surroundings and act appropriately.

Action: Ask everyone to clean up, and then start cleaning up yourself along with your colleagues when everyone else has finished. This approach is also applicable to a variety of other jobs.

The third most important aspect of leadership is having an influence.

Taking this into consideration, it ought to have a positive influence. Someone showing up to their place of employment with the intention of challenging their authority is something I've seen far too often, and it has a detrimental impact on the atmosphere there. They did have an effect, but it was a negative one on the world.

I once worked for a boss who, as soon as he assumed leadership of a new location, sat everyone down, let us take a drink, removed his rank slip, and then proceeded to have a debate lasting between two and three hours regarding the positive and negative aspects of the location. Because of this, he was able to get all of the responses he required from his staff members, as well as a great deal of respect from everyone involved in the process.

Action: Try this out at your place of employment. Gather everyone together, and have an open forum discussion about the positive aspects and negative aspects of your workplace that need to be improved. There should be no ramifications for anything that is stated during these sessions.

Understanding Leadership is the Topic of Leadership 101.

The first thing we need to do is have a better grasp on what leadership really entails before we can go on to discussing actionable methods and pointers that may help you become a great leader who is also able to influence the behavior of others around you. The approaches and pointers that were presented will make more sense after you have a firm grasp on the concept of true leadership.

The concept of leadership is one that is often misunderstood. In point of fact, the vast majority of people believe that leadership is all about superiority and domination. While it is true that leadership may be achieved via the use of force, this style of leadership is neither sustainable, ethical, or acceptable. In this book, we will be talking about how to build the attributes of a leader that others will respect and naturally WANT to follow. This is the topic that will be covered.

You should make learning a lifelong activity and read as much as you can on any subject that interests you, including the issue of leadership. There are many wonderful gurus out there who can go into great depth about all of the ways in which you may be a great leader. I urge you to make learning a lifelong affair and study as much as you can on any topic that interests you. However, in this article, we are going to provide you with a condensed version of the information necessary to become an excellent leader. Do not be misled by the shortness of this book; the knowledge contained inside these pages has the potential to transform your standing within any group dynamic into that of a leader, provided that you use it in a consistent manner.

Who Are the People Who Lead?

As opposed to what is often believed, being a leader involves a great deal more than just having the highest position in a company or being the one who issues directives to others. It is possible to hold a position of authority while simultaneously lacking the self-assurance, experience, and personality traits necessary to motivate people to willingly cooperate with one another toward the accomplishment of a shared objective in order to reach a successful conclusion.

Who, therefore, has the role of a leader? Someone who keeps their promise is the definition of a leader. A competent leader is one who is also fair and has an open mind. A real leader would never ask followers to do anything that they themselves wouldn't be willing to undertake. A leader is someone who recognizes when something needs to be done and then does it on their own without being asked. A good leader is one who is always willing to learn and to teach others. A good leader is compassionate and inspiring to others around them. A good leader fights with his team, accepts responsibility for the losses that the team suffers, and provides credit to his team for any successes that they achieve. A leader is someone whose words, actions, and body language have a positive impact on others to the point that they feel forced to put in their best effort to keep things functioning. This compels others to follow the leader's example and provide their best efforts to the success of the endeavor.

If you work toward attaining the attributes described above, other people will naturally WANT to follow your lead. When you employ coercion as a form of leadership, your followers will not respect you, productivity will be at an all-time low, and the dynamic of the workplace will be unpleasant. This is not leadership; rather, it is acting in a supervisory capacity. Continue reading this article if you want to build a long-lasting leadership position that is founded on the respect and believe of people in you.

It is true that the characteristics of a successful leader might seem like a large order to fulfill, but I want you to know that you shouldn't worry about it since with enough practice, those characteristics will become second nature to you. It is NEVER too late to begin developing into the person you have ALWAYS DREAMED of becoming. What we present to the outside world is a picture of ourselves that we've concocted based on our surroundings, our upbringing, our education, our self-image, the values that we hold, and the beliefs that we have. Once you are conscious of this fact, you will be able to begin the process of developing new convictions and principles, as well as altering the kind of personality you have.

Now that you have a better grasp of what it takes to be a leader, we will go a bit more into how to develop and put these abilities and attributes into practice so that you may become a successful leader.

Know Your Leadership Style is the Topic of Chapter 1

The first step in becoming a successful leader is figuring out what sort of leader one already is. There are essentially four distinct kinds of leaders, and they are all on an even playing field. The only thing that differentiates them is how they carry out their leadership and how well they can connect with other people. These categories are as follows:

Leaders with the Courage to Lead. Even when confronted with a difficult situation, individuals like this never lose sight of their long-term objectives and vision. They are aware of their goals, and they understand how to uphold the principles that guide them. In this day and age, it is necessary to learn how to be true to yourself and how to stick to your gut because it is basically what you will have left, amidst all the changes. It is important to learn how to be true to yourself and how to stick to your gut because it is basically what you will have left. People will come to the conclusion that you are someone who is worthy of being emulated if you are able to maintain your authenticity.

Leaders Who Are Servants. If you have a high level of concern for the people you supervise, you are most likely the servant-type of leader. They often inquire about how they may be of assistance to others and frequently consider ways in which things might be improved upon and altered. They don't simply sit in the office and delegate everything out to others; rather of doing that, they get their hands dirty with whatever it is that has to be done. In addition to thinking, this shows that they are proactive. They are also kind and charitable, and they are willing to assist others in any manner that they can.

Leaders who can inspire others. Inspirational leaders are leaders who are devoted to their beliefs and values and who can motivate others to do the same. They inspire others to think that positive change is possible and that if they put their minds and souls into something, they will be able to accomplish what they set out to do. They often exhibit new thinking and a focus on the future. They don't accept the existence of limits and maintain the mindset that the opportunities are limitless. They do not conform to the present; rather, they focus on the future and consider what they may do to influence it.

Influential Thinkers. Leaders of thought make use of their brains and have the mindset that they can always improve their knowledge as long as they continue to live. They open people's eyes to the fact that education does not end in the classroom and that there is a great deal more about the world that each and every person need to be aware of. They earn the increased respect of those who follow them by demonstrating to them that change is possible and that they have the potential to do great things for themselves and the world. People adore them because of the change they are able to bring about in the world.

So, tell me about the sort of leader you are.

Keep in mind that it is essential to determine the sort of leader you are so that you may have more conviction as a person and, as a result, have greater influence on those who report to you. If you have a strong sense of self-identity, it will be difficult for others to knock you down, and it will be simple for you to serve as an example to others around you. If you are aware of who you are, you will have a far better chance of doing the things you set out to do.

Always Aim Before You Jump.

If you have ten teams working on a single project, you have the possibility for 10,000 different project plans. Anything that has to be done may be done in more than one manner. Favorite techniques may range from excellent to awful, optimistic to pessimistic, achievable to impossible, brilliant to, well... not so brilliant, and so on and so forth, depending on the specific abilities, preferences, experiences, and personalities of the people using them. The successful leader is able to rally the support and involvement of the team behind an effective strategy. This approach does not have to be the "best" approach (because there are no ideal plans), nor does it have to be anyone's "favorite" approach (as my way is seldom the team way). Leaders who get their core teams involved in developing a work breakdown structure (WBS) for the project are already one step ahead of the competition. It has already been agreed upon, negotiated, and debated which options and methods will be taken. If you've made it this far in the book without a comprehensive checklist of activities and benchmarks, STOP! It is definitely not the right moment to leap from the roof! Go back and try to get an agreement on a strategy as well as the activities and actions that are necessary for it. Keep in mind that the quality of the WBS will determine the quality of every consequence from this point forward: a poor list equals a bad plan equals terrible outcomes.

It is simple to proceed with the incorrect WBS; any one of us is capable of being caught off guard. Everyone runs the risk of being taken advantage of by the clichéd "unknown unknowns." And after you've taken the plunge into execution, changing paths in the middle of the air is not always an option. That requires the kind of superpowers that are exclusive to Marvel Comics. For the time being, I'm going to continue our planning conversation on the premise that either you already have a decent task list (made by the individuals who will be performing the work), or you're going to produce one before moving on to the next phase, which is scheduling the work.

Before you dive headfirst into this project and try to move things along as rapidly as you can, you need to make sure that every member of your team is aware of their tasks and is dedicated to carrying them out. I know you're excited to get started, but before you do that, you need to make sure that everyone is on the same page. The process of creating a work breakdown structure has provided you and the essential members of the team with a fairly good notion of who is going to be doing what, but at this stage, you need to get specific: precisely who is going to do exactly what, and exactly when they are going to do it. The goal of the leader is to clarify everyone's duties and responsibilities in greater detail. Make sure that every member of the team is aware of their duties, responsibilities, and expected deadline for outcomes. This step may seem little, but it is really necessary. Facilitating Clarity of Action is a leadership tool that helps leaders reinforce Purpose and foster Enthusiasm among their team members.

To ensure that all members of the team are on the same page during a short project or in an environment in which they routinely collaborate, some extra effort in terms of preparation and communication may be required. An strategy that is more sophisticated and resilient is necessary when dealing with bigger projects that include a higher number of people, a greater level of complexity, or an unclear understanding of how activities are connected. This chapter will mostly concentrate on the topic. As a leader, I have no doubt that you are familiar with the proverb, "For some people, you just have to draw them a picture."

Accountability As Well As Availability For Contact

Being accountable involves taking responsibility for your actions when life compels you to. This is something that a leader does without even consciously considering it. It's very normal, and it just goes along with the territory. People are able to contact the leader in order to make him more aware of difficulties, and as a result, the leader is in a position to utilize all of the knowledge at his disposal in order to construct new bridges that lead to the future. The issue here is that unsuccessful leaders have a propensity to point the blame upon others.

Due to the fact that he is in control, a leader is always held accountable for the actions of his workforce or team at the end of the day. As a consequence of this, he is responsible for the outcomes that are achieved by the team. Even if just one member of the team is ineffective, the blame should be placed on the leadership since there is no question that the leadership was the one who committed the error of hiring individuals who were not sufficiently knowledgeable to carry out the duties of the job correctly. No matter how you look at it, the leader is to blame, and a good leader recognizes this fact and adds his or her personal responsibility to the larger picture of how to recover from a challenging circumstance.

When it comes to being a leader, being approachable is one of the most important habits to have. If the individuals who work for you are unwilling to approach you and tell you their concerns, then those concerns will continue to build up. When this occurs, you are not aware that there are difficulties, and the repercussions of problems that have built up over time might be more severe than the consequences of problems that have just surfaced and have had your insight into them. Being approachable also implies that others who follow in your footsteps will look up to you as an example. They have the impression that you are the "go to" person if they want to discuss anything, and this includes enhancements in techniques, which might result in significant cost savings.

Those managers who try to put themselves apart from their employees by establishing a hierarchy in which personnel are expected to remain in the roles that have been assigned to them seldom fare very well professionally. They are unable of seeing the bigger picture since they rely only on themselves. The leader may have a far more comprehensive perspective on the situation by holding frequent meetings with the team and encouraging everyone to share their opinions.

individuals who are able to make others around them feel at ease are the kind of individuals that make excellent leaders. In a report that was published online, a student who had the opportunity to speak with Bill Gates described how anxious she was about the encounter, given that she was given the chance to do so. When he introduced himself as "Bill," he instantly opened up a channel of warmth that was noted right away. This made her feel both humbled and a bit anxious about the concept. Because she was interested in learning more about Bill Gates, she decided to watch the guy. Elynn Lee, a worker at UTCS, was startled to find out how friendly Bill Gates was. In addition to this, she saw something else about him that caught her attention. He was a guy of few words who spent most of his time listening and watching his surroundings in silence, absorbing everything in. Being an engaged listener is one of the most effective ways for entrepreneurs, according to other businesspeople, to grow their own knowledge sets. This is but one illustration of the many ways in which individuals make themselves accessible.

They develop their ability to listen carefully and are open to engaging in conversation with others of diverse ages and backgrounds. This kid picked up on the fact that Bill Gates did not behave in an arrogant manner more than anything else. He did not interrupt individuals in the middle of their sentences or attempt to correct what they were saying. Potential leaders who behave in this manner have a lower likelihood of gaining a reputation for being accessible, and there is a very excellent rationale for this phenomenon. You distance yourself from other people and make yourself less accessible when you have the mindset that the viewpoint that you are listening to is less significant than the one that you are forming in your own head. People are more likely to be scared away by your presence than to be encouraged by it, which means that you effectively eliminate any possibility of effective dialogue.

On the same website, other people who had something to say about Bill Gates stated things that amounted to the same thing. The individual was very easy to talk to, kind, and willing to provide answers to any questions that were posed. When you make yourself more accessible, you provide other people the opportunity to learn your thoughts on issues concerning the significance of issues that are important to them. Amazingly, he was able to answer questions on the spot, and strong leaders don't mind being confronted even at a moment's notice because they have the conviction to stand up for what they believe in and don't feel the need to hide behind jargon.

They are aware that it is their responsibility to be responsible, and they are also aware that being accessible is beneficial to the cause that they are fighting for. These behaviors are both natural to a great kickass leader and will hold him in high respect because people appreciate the fact that they haven't allowed their heights of success stand in the way of meeting those of lower or higher status. In other words, people admire the fact that they haven't let their heights of success stand in the way of meeting those of weaker or greater status. They are also aware that they owe individuals a certain amount of duty, and they are prepared to go above and beyond in order to demonstrate that they take that obligation seriously. Accountability demonstrates to the outside world that you are not scared to stick by your views, and approachability assists in maintaining the compatibility of your values with the events that are taking place in the world around you. For this reason, moguls in the IT industry actually do create fantastic examples for others to follow. They pay attention to what customers want, take what they say into consideration, and then develop goods that fulfill those requirements. These are the kind of leaders whose accomplishments may serve as models for others.

Increasing One's Self-Assurance While At Work

After addressing the fundamental causes of your lack of self-confidence, it is time to turn your attention to the professional environment in which you find yourself. It's possible that many individuals feel self-assured outside of the job, but as soon as they step foot in the office, their nerves take over and they completely lose their self-assurance. This is due to the fact that the environment of the workplace may be frightening, which in turn can drive an individual to overthink what they are doing. The cumulative effect of all of this negative energy is to limit your potential since it becomes a mass.

You are going to learn how to handle various scenarios that may arise at work, as well as how to cultivate a confident manner in order to effectively address the challenges that are specific to the working environment.

Confronting Your Own Self-Doubt

Self-doubt is something that affects all of us, and although it is typically controllable, if we attempt to deny it, it just becomes worse. Self-doubt has the ability to destroy whatever confidence we may have, and the best way to deal with it when you hear that critical voice in your brain is to ignore it and take action to stop it from gaining control of your thinking. Because of this fear, the idea continues to get more powerful, and it becomes more difficult to ignore; this is why it keeps coming back, slowly draining all of your energy and leaving you feeling emotionally drained as a result.

You have to confront these pessimistic ideas head-on and do it with self-assurance. There is no way that you will be able to come into work and deal with criticism or anybody challenging you if you are unable to manage the bad energy that is already circulating inside you. When you take the time to handle all of your self-doubts in advance, you guarantee that it will be much less probable for anything similar to affect you when it is brought up by another person. This is because you will have previously dealt with it in your thoughts.

Self-doubt may also shed light on the many concerns we have over our profession, and by addressing these concerns, all you are doing is preparing yourself for work the following day. Therefore, if a voice within your head is convincing you that your presentation is going to bomb the next day, you should focus even more energy on perfecting it over the evening. Perfect every part of it to ensure that there is no room for criticism. This will provide you with the additional assurance that you can only acquire when the quality of your job meets or exceeds expectations. Nothing else can offer you the feeling of self-assurance that you get from doing more study only to make sure that you are over-prepared for everything that may be asked during the meeting.

When you are confronted with uncertainty, all you need to do is redirect your attention back to what you already know and what you can be certain of. Doubt might give us the impression that we are not in control of the situation and that everything is heading in the wrong direction, but if you depend on the information you already possess, you will begin to feel more grounded.

Get Rid of the Triggers

There are some triggers in our lives that might cause us to relive painful experiences, and these memories have the power to render us immobile. Because we comprehend everything via association, some individuals and locations are permanently imprinted in our brains with negative connotations. This is because we understand everything through association. If you have ever been made to feel ashamed or degraded at work, you will always associate going to work with those negative emotions. If this has happened to you, you may avoid going to work altogether. So, what steps can you take to fix the problem?

The first thing you need to do is get rid of these triggers. If at all possible, stay away from them and try not to face them directly. On the other hand, you can't constantly avoid your triggers, and at some time, you will have no choice but to confront them. You are able to conquer your triggers if you just learn to regulate the response you have to them. You just need to rethink the link you have with certain locations or individuals in order to prevent seeing them from causing you to be reminded of unpleasant experiences. If someone reprimanded you at work, you should take that person out for ice cream so that the bad connection you have formed with this person may be turned into a pleasant one, which will negate the discomfort caused by the first reprimand.

Recognize the Gifts You Have.

You were selected for this position because you have a unique quality and you were already familiar with the duties involved. You just need to have faith in yourself and what you're capable of, and everything else will fall into place. We all have the experience of feeling as if we are simply putting on an act when it comes to something that we are not very knowledgeable about. It is known as imposter syndrome, and it is a mental state that may be defined by continually underestimating and questioning your abilities and expertise and instead feeling that you are only pretending to know things. Imposter syndrome is a mental condition that can be characterized by these features. The best way to get rid of this condition is to acknowledge the special skills that you possess. It does not have to be a really significant item. One of the most valuable skills one may possess is the ability to comprehend other people's perspectives and motivations. You have to come to terms with the fact that you possess these admirable and uplifting qualities.

Allow for Some Unclearness

When we wait for solutions and they don't come to us right away, we have a tendency to feel dissatisfied, which leads us to condemn ourselves. Therefore, when it is required of you to make a choice and you can't think of the correct responses, try to look at the situation as an opportunity rather than a setback.

There is a lack of assurance, which suggests that there must be something about the decision-making process that isn't quite right. Because of this, there is ambiguity, which occurs because of this lack of confidence. Acquaint yourself with the concept of ambiguity as an intuitive inquiry of what to do and how to proceed. The uncertainty will provide you with questions, and those questions are what will bring you to answers. If you have doubts about anything, you should first investigate the reasons behind such doubts, and then go from there. If you start to believe that you should have answers right away without even addressing the issues that are now running through your brain, then the expectations that you have placed on yourself will ultimately lead to your failure.

The Crucial Aspect Is Confrontation

People who lack confidence try to please other people and desire the approval that comes from doing so, which is why they constantly behave in a polite manner. Now, although this may be successful outside of the workplace, in order to be successful inside, you need to have a harsh exterior at times. Because you didn't address your unease with anything, the connections you create with other people at work won't be as solid if you don't approach them about the things that make you uncomfortable. Confronting other people about the things that upset you and not being frightened of having uncomfortable talks are essential components of having confidence.

Although it may seem to be unproductive at the time, at the end of the day, when the conversation is finished, you will have a connection that is much more honest with your coworkers and subordinates. You should never ignore a problem that exists between you and another coworker in the job and instead actively seek out methods to solve it.

This is also very important since having confidence implies not being scared to be questioned by other people. By facing challenges from other people, you will learn how to stand up for yourself even when others are doubting what you are doing or saying. You shouldn't take it personally; rather, you should regard it as valuable input that will assist you in rethinking your leadership approach.

A Formula For Quicker Results As A Framework

You must be able to persuade other individuals to work toward the common objectives of the group in order to fulfill the requirements of the definition of leadership that I presented previously in this book. The term that best describes this situation is "influence," and the easiest way to explain influence is to say that its meaning is "to get a willing yes." To convince somebody to say 'yes,' you can use force, but I consider that to be manipulation. You can also beg or bribe them, but I consider those to be forms of persuasion rather than manipulation.

When I was talking about leadership in the past, I used driving as a metaphor. If you have ever driven a vehicle with a manual gearbox, sometimes known as a "stick shift," you are familiar with the sensation of utilizing the clutch and changing gears in a fluid manner. You probably likely know how it feels to press the gears while driving and have the vehicle fight back against you.

Smooth may be achieved at any speed, even slow.

—Seals of the United States Navy

This phrase, said by a group that engages in some of the riskiest activities in the world, serves as an excellent reminder to take one's time and do one's responsibilities well.

You will be expected to generate results in your role as a leader; but, if you keep things running smoothly and keep your team engaged, you may achieve results more quickly.

The New Leadership Framework was one of the topics that I covered when I spoke about the reasons why you should read this book.

The mentality and motivation of an individual may be favorably influenced by clear expectations, which in turn can impact the appropriate actions that lead to quicker outcomes.

This way of thinking has a multiplying effect and, if carried out correctly, will make it possible for you to scale not just your results but also your team and your whole business.

On the other hand, you and your team will fail to meet your goals (also known as "crash and burn") if you do not establish clear expectations, if individuals do not have the appropriate attitude, and if their actions do not line with the ideals of the organization.

Specific Goals and Objectives

We have made the decision to send humans to the moon within this decade in addition to achieving our other goals not because they are simple but rather because they are challenging. We have made this decision because we believe that achieving this goal will allow us to better organize and evaluate the entirety of our efforts and capabilities. Furthermore, we believe that this challenge is one that we are willing to accept, one that we are unwilling to postpone, and one that we intend to win in addition to achieving our other goals.

— John F. Kennedy, President of the United States

In September of 1962, President John F. Kennedy gave his now-famous address, "We Choose to Go to the Moon," in front of an audience of around 40,000 people. The Russian astronaut Yuri Gagarin had successfully completed an orbit of the earth the year before, and this caused the United States to be terrified of the Soviet Union's domination in space.

The speech was significant for a number of reasons, not the least of which was the fact that at the time it was given, NASA was still months away from successfully sending a man into space and had no clue how they would accomplish this aim. Kennedy mobilized attitudes and behaviors that finally led to American astronaut Neil Armstrong setting foot on the moon on July 20, 1969. He did this by setting large and clear expectations for what was to come.

Do you, as a manager and a leader, establish clear and high expectations for your employees?

First, you make it very apparent to everyone what outcomes you want them to produce. After then, you talk about how to achieve those outcomes. (2002) (Bossidy)

Have you ever given someone a task or a request and then asked them, "Do you understand?" after you gave them the responsibility? It's quite likely that you have, and the normal response that people give is 'Yes.' However, did they get the concept? It's possible that not. So, why does anything like this occur?

Miscommunication occurs when you have an expectation in your brain, and when other people listen to you, they attempt to fit what they hear into an expectation they already have. This leads to misunderstandings. They answer "yes" because they comprehend the situation from their perspective, which may or may not align with yours.

Thinking about it:

Consider a piece of work that you assigned but the results of which did not live up to your expectations. How could you have stated your question in a clearer manner?

Surprisingly, asking questions is more important than providing direct answers when it comes to establishing clear expectations. Asking questions such as "What is important about this?" is an effective way to create appropriate expectations.

• What steps should we take to solve this problem?

• What would be the appropriate action to take?

You may learn how a person has framed their future behaviors by asking them questions about those activities. If, however, you feel the need to explain things in further depth, make it a point to question the individual's level of comprehension by asking whether or not they just comprehend the work at hand.

It is possible for you to create the expectation that an employee would buy a couch; but, is this a clear expectation?

Obviously not, given that couches are available in a wide range of dimensions, hues, and fabrics, not to mention pricing points. You could explain each of these criteria in your request, or you could be explicit about where and how you want to utilize the couch (for example, in the client waiting area), and then ask your employee if they are comfortable making the pick based on the outcome you are looking for. Either way, you will need to make sure that you have all of the necessary information.

PAUSE AND CONSIDER

How well do you understand your own vision, as well as the underlying beliefs and guiding principles of the people you are responsible for leading?

How may you lead with more transparency and steadiness in your approach?

It is not always simple to be a clear, well-defined, and consistent leader in today's high-pressure workplace, when leaders may be pushed off course by the numerous competing, and sometimes contradictory, demands they must confront. However, it is essential for leaders to be able to do so in order to be successful.

The Tale of Tom

Bridgette counseled Tom, the head of a very successful family-owned firm that was in negotiations with another organization interested in either a merger or a buyout, a number of years ago. The conversations were taking place during this time. The discussions were intended to be held in the strictest confidence; yet, thanks to leaks from the other group, it had become general knowledge, and worry was building across Tom's firm about the possibility that job cuts or substantial layoffs may be the outcome.

Tom was a man of strong principles and had a profound dedication to his staff of devoted workers. Even though he had no intention of reaching an agreement that would include firing employees, he had pledged to keep the fact that negotiations were even taking place a secret from anybody who may ask about it. He was also aware of how detrimental it was to allow the unjustified concerns of his staff to continue to propagate among them and elevate their level of worry even more. Tom also understood his responsibility to support the emotional health of the system, and in what was a very bold move in the midst of the delicate talks, he halted the process and renegotiated his confidentiality agreement to allow him to (1) acknowledge to his employees that talks were underway that could potentially bring great benefit to their company and (2) reassure his employees that the talks were about growth possibilities, and that layoffs were not part of any of the discussions that were taking place. Tom also understood that he had a responsibility to support the

He conveyed those two ideas to his staff in a manner that might have made him the poster child for our Second Big Idea. He did it in a way that was both calm and with a great deal of conviction. Tom had worked hard over the course of many years to acquire the profound confidence of his colleagues. As a result, when he assured them that their jobs were not in immediate danger, they trusted him and accepted his word at face value. Because of this, there was a significant decrease in worry, a change in the atmosphere of the organization, and a spike in productivity as his staff stepped up its performance to demonstrate what a wonderful firm they worked for.

It does not matter what rank you hold within the business; it is essential to demonstrate clear leadership that is well-defined and consistent. It doesn't matter whether you are the CEO of a company or a first-time supervisor; when you communicate your vision, values, and guiding principles, you assist people understand what they may expect from you as well as what you expect from them.

The Third Huge Concept: An Innovative Approach to LEADING:

Maintain your line of action in the face of opposition and sabotage, but do it without feeling the need to be defensive or triumph.

Bob was called upon by one of his old customers, Annette, who wanted his assistance in remaining thoughtful while leading a very difficult change-management program that she had been appointed to oversee. The board of directors of a high-tech business had selected her to serve as CEO with the explicit directive to "change the company culture." Prior to her hiring, the company was extremely compartmentalized, with an excessive amount of internal competitiveness and an insufficient amount of cooperation or communication between departments. Annette's hiring occurred at the same time as a long-planned transfer of the corporate headquarters, and she had already made up her mind to take use of the opportunity presented by the move to send a clear message that silos would no longer be permitted to remain in place.

When Bob initially met with her, she was far into the process of implementing her plan, which required building a cutting-edge office environment in which no one, not even the top leadership team, had their own private office space. Annette had used the motto "No more closed doors" to indicate to the members of her leadership team that they were being tasked with engaging in a degree of cooperation and cross-division communication that would kick-start a more inventive and agile reset of the organizational culture. "No more closed doors" was the mantra that Annette had employed.

During the very first coaching session that Annette and Bob had together, Annette vented her frustration to Bob over two specific members of her team. Both had been expressing their disapproval of the new workplace arrangement to everyone else except Annette in a subdued manner, often closing their statements with a gloomy "There's no way this crazy idea will work!" She confided in Bob her feeling of betrayal at their disloyalty and that she was going to call them out at the next meeting of the senior team, which she had scheduled for the following morning in her office, despite the fact that the next meeting that was regularly scheduled would not take place for another two weeks. Her tone was tense as she said this. In her conversation with Bob, she said, "I will not have sabotage!"

What exactly is going on over here?

When leaders try to lead change, they often share their experiences with us, and Annette's narrative is representative of many of those experiences. They will inevitably run with opposition that seems to be purposeful sabotage, and when this happens, they often find themselves at a loss for how to react. What can we possibly take away from the scenario involving Annette if we examine her responses, as well as the responses of her team, through the lens of resilient leadership? The following are some thoughts that should be taken into consideration:

An action or stance that you take that charts a new direction for you, your team, and/or your organization that is based on a serious examination of your vision, values, and guiding principles is considered a self-differentiating move. You may think of it as a move that you do to chart a new course.

We refer to Annette's choice to significantly restructure the office environment as a "self-differentiating move," the same term we use to describe what Bill and Tom did in the First Big Idea and the Second Big Idea, respectively. These kinds of maneuvers are very necessary for leading with conviction, and for a leader to pull them off successfully, they need not just a great lot of clarity but also a high level of executional prowess.

It is nearly certain that a self-differentiating action made by a leader will be met with opposition (sabotage), most often coming from the portions of the system that are not as effectively differentiated. This is the case because, by definition, the purpose of systems is to preserve the status quo, even in circumstances when change is desperately required.

'Such sabotage often seems highly personal, as it did to Annette (after all, the poison arrows seemed to be pointed directly at her), and she became hooked into responding without stopping to observe her own concern or to moderate her own fearful reaction. 'Such sabotage often feels deeply personal, as it did to Annette.

Because of her emotional sensitivity, Annette became hyper-focused on silencing the dissidents rather than clarifying her position in a composed and authoritative manner.

Setting A Course Of Action And A Vision Are Both Essential Components Of Effective Leadership.

A person is considered to be a leader when they are the one on whom the whole group leans upon in order to go on their path toward achievement. If a leader is the kind of person who is unable to establish objectives, then that person can never be considered a genuine leader. On the other hand, a person who has the potential to become a leader might also be a regular person who will carry out all of the commendable deeds that are required of him. A good leader is someone who not only has the attitude of goal-setting but also has a crystal clear vision of what it is that he is accomplishing. A guy from the common class who has the capacity to create goals may develop into an exceptional leader. If a leader is unable to direct followers toward desirable outcomes, it is time for him to step aside and let someone else take the helm. A good leader is one who has a clear vision for the future, not just for himself but also for the people he is leading beside him.

A leader who lacks vision is comparable to a ship that has no one to steer it. If an average person can demonstrate that he is capable of establishing goals for himself and moving forward in accordance with those goals, then that person has the potential to lead. Take, for instance:

Example A: There is no one designated as the team captain and a guy is going to participate in a football game nevertheless. The catch is that whomever performs the best will be promoted to the role of captain for the remaining games of the season. During the game, a guy shown his ability to achieve something positive in the face of intense pressure, and he demonstrated remarkable talents in order to come out on top. However, he conducted the work in a way more consistent with that of an amateur than a professional.

The issue at hand is this: should he be thought of as the kind of person who would make a suitable captain for the team? Or should there be another competition to choose who would lead the squad as captain?

Even if the individual did not play in a professional way, the correct response is that he ought to be selected as the captain of the team. The most important reason for this is that he is able to demonstrate great goal-setting abilities in addition to having a solid vision. He and his squad would never have had a chance of winning the game if they didn't have a specific plan to follow. Therefore, in this scenario, he ought to be selected to serve as the captain.

He has a mind that is both acute and smart, making him a guy who has the potential to raise the quality of leadership to the next level. Yesterday, he may have been a regular guy, but today he has shown that he is more than capable of leading. This is due to the fact that he not only had strong foresight in the direction of doing something, but also did an excellent job of working his way into the good graces of a large number of people despite the intense amount of competition.

A leader may encourage his team by encouraging the individual's thinking, as well as by explaining his goal in straightforward language. Even an average individual is capable of doing this and rising to the position of leader by transforming themselves from the follower they were yesterday into a person with the ability to establish goals. He has the potential to become a great leader in the future as well as a prospective leader in the present.

In addition to that, he will be performing an excellent job by correctly carrying out his responsibilities and elevating his obligation to an entirely new level. In order for him to become a good leader, he is going to start appreciating and embracing the responsibilities he has. Because of this, in order for him to transition from being a follower to a leader, he will need to aim as high as he possibly can. He will also be a guy with excellent leadership skills, which will aid him in team building with his new leadership and goal setting abilities. Additionally, he will be a man with strong leadership skills.

If the capacity to define goals is something that even an average person can have, then anybody can rise to the position of leader. Even if he has not yet achieved the position of leader despite possessing such talents, he undoubtedly has the attributes necessary to achieve that position in the future. Therefore, it is clear that he is on the path to become a leader in the future.

If an everyday person asserts that he is capable of understanding the thoughts and actions of other people, then that individual has the potential to become a future leader. As we have seen, a guy in a leadership position who lacks vision is almost worthless. In the same vein, a man who has a vision is on par with a leader. If a guy has these traits of having a great vision and fantastic goal setting abilities, then it must be understood that he has the potential to be a leader. If he does not have these qualities, then he does not have the potential to be a leader. To demonstrate his worth as a leader, all he needs is some direction and support, which he already has.

One should simply possess a bright intellect in order to have the capacity to create objectives not just for oneself but also for one's team. If you are capable of establishing objectives not just for yourself but also for other people, you not only have a smart intellect but also have the potential to become a leader in the future. It is quite evident that you have the potential to be a leader, and more specifically, a great leader, if you have the vision both for yourself and for your team.

Therefore, in order to become a great leader, all that is required of you is the capacity to think beyond what you already know and to see beyond your own way of thinking. It means to envisage things that are beyond even the most advanced degree of your mind. If you possess each of these traits, then you are the one who is meant to become an outstanding leader. You are the only one who can prevent you from carrying this through.

The Demonstration Of Leadership Requires Consistency.

Leaders that are consistent always act with honesty and fairness in everything they undertake. Dependability and dependability are hallmarks of strong leaders. They keep their word and fulfill all of their obligations. At the same time, they indicate the expectation that each individual member of the team will follow through on the obligations that are specifically assigned to them. Self-reflection is a common trait shared by exceptional leaders. They are aware of their fallibility as humans and acknowledge the possibility of making errors. When they do make a mistake, rather of placing blame on others, they take responsibility for it and move on. Great leaders are also aware that the accomplishments of the whole team are directly proportional to their own, and as a result, they take equal credit for the achievements of the group.

Loyalty is fostered by strong leaders. Having said that, loyalty works both ways. I am not referring to the unquestioning allegiance that some inept leaders assume they are entitled to just because of their position. I am referring to a dedication that everyone on the team has in common to the goals that the team has set. The members of the team strive towards the objectives set by the leader because their goals are congruent with the goals set by the leader. It's possible that attempting to lead via intimidation and terror may work for a short period of time, but it's not a method that will function over the long term. There will be uprisings among the followers, as well as acts of sabotage, and many of the most talented will abandon the cause. Disloyalty is bred in an environment where there is a culture of fear. Many new leaders make the common error of erroneously believing that the members of their team would immediately respect them just because of their job title or position of power. It is necessary for a leader to get the respect of their team.

It is unrealistic to assume that the members of your team would gladly follow you merely because of your position in the business. Respect is the foundation for loyalty. When you initially take on the role of leader, you get this knowledge. You decide on a work plan for the workers but do not discuss with them beforehand. By doing so, you are ignoring the qualities that set one member of staff apart from the others. Some staff members are quite effective in their work at the front desk, but they struggle more when it comes to providing assistance to customers. Other staff members are excellent with customers but have a more difficult time preparing food. When scheduling, you failed to take into account the capabilities and limitations of the staff members, which caused the whole operation to struggle for a while. Employees are upset, morale is poor, and both our efficiency and our ability to provide good service to customers are suffering as a result. A number of important workers resigned.

You don't become aware of your error until a staff meeting in which you pose the question to the workers, "What could we change to become more effective?" You were taken aback by their responses, which revealed that they were dissatisfied with your leadership because they believed you were failing to make the most of their abilities. You took what was said into consideration and altered the scheduling procedure. Both morale and productivity went up when the workers were given the opportunity to have input on the timetable. Your connection with the staff will quickly develop into one based on mutual respect if you continue to treat them with dignity and courtesy.

Honor your obligations and commitments.

How can strong leaders show that they are consistent in their actions? They accomplish this goal by means of both their words and their deeds. They are reliable in that once they make a promise to accomplish something, they stick to that commitment. Be careful to keep your end of the bargain if your team agrees that you will bring up an issue with your supervisor about the need for extra resources and you then fail to follow through and take the problem up with your supervisor. You will find that during the course of your career, you will often be asked to take a request to top management despite the fact that you are very convinced that the request would be refused.

The most essential thing is that you stick to the terms of the promise you made. These petitions are often turned down, just as you anticipated they would be, but every once in a while they are granted. You are able to go back to the team in an honest manner and offer a report on the outcomes, regardless of the conclusion of the situation. You have the position of manager at a company and are notorious for not following through on commitments of this kind. You would not even bother taking the request to your supervisor if you believed it would not be granted. You should just return to the team and explain to them that the request cannot be fulfilled at this time. Some of the other members of the team will eventually find out that you are not following through with the tasks assigned to you and that you are lying when you pretend that you have completed them. In the end, the group descends into disorder and becomes incapable of functioning as a unit. The purpose of the squad is never really completed, and as a result, the unit finally disbands.

Make the members of the team responsible for their actions.

Another component of commitment is making sure that you follow through on the promises that other members of the team make to you and ensuring that you do so in a timely manner. They are required to demonstrate accountability to you and the other members of the team for the successful accomplishment of the work, regardless of whether they volunteered for the responsibility or were allocated it. This starts with making sure that your expectations are not muddled in any way. Inquire with them as to whether or not they are aware of the commitments they are making. Don't accept a straightforward "yes" as the correct response. Ask them to state it once again but this time in their own words. It is also a very good idea to explain to them how you would follow up with them to make sure that they completed the pledge that they made. Do you need frequent updates on the progress of your project? Are you planning to do an analysis of quantitative data? There is no way for you to hold the members of the team responsible for the contributions that they made to the team if adequate follow up is not performed. The performance should be evaluated in a neutral and impartial manner throughout the review process. You are sending a message to the member of the team that this task is essential and that you will hold them responsible for accomplishing it if you implement an assessment mechanism.

The manner in which you follow up is of the utmost importance, particularly in situations in which a member of the team is not meeting the objectives that were agreed to. Investigating the reasons why the objectives are not being accomplished is necessary, as is determining if more resources are required. Is the timetable completely unrealistic? You will establish a relationship based on trust with your teammates if you keep the promises that you make to them and if you keep the obligations that other members of the team make to you. The loyalty of the members of your team will increase if you, as the leader, can show that you can be counted on and that you will see things through to the end. When you demonstrate that you can be relied upon, others will be more willing to do the same for you.

Self-reflection is an Essential Skill for Successful Leaders

Successful leaders have a firm grasp on who they are. They are aware of the activities in which they excel. They are also aware of the constraints that they face. Nobody is exceptional in every aspect of their life. While some of us are skilled planners, others are more adept at carrying out the strategies laid forth in the plan. Some of us are more skilled than others when it comes to engaging in linguistic exchanges. You must always be truthful with yourself because it is the most essential thing.

Learning how to evaluate the strengths and shortcomings of the members of the team is another skill that is essential. To begin, you should have every member of the team evaluate themselves. What do they consider to be some of their greatest strengths? In most cases, individuals of the team will be eager to discuss the skills they bring to the table. Understand that questioning them about their constraints will not provide the same level of positive results. Some of them will be honest and discuss what they believe to be limits, but most of the time, we feel uncomfortable talking about our own restrictions in public. Listening to and observing the other members of the team will provide you with a wealth of information about them. Pay close attention to how they communicate with the other members of the team. Do they have a strong written voice, or do they communicate more effectively verbally? Do they seem to be more at ease in an official situation, such as a meeting, or do they do better in a more intimate setting, such as a one-on-one conversation?

Great leaders are also aware that the activities taken by the whole of the team are directly proportional to the success that they enjoy. When the team is successful, the credit is distributed evenly among them. They are willing to take responsibility for their errors and will readily acknowledge when they are in the wrong. Leaders that are consistent always act with honesty and fairness in everything they undertake. Dependability and dependability are hallmarks of strong leaders. They keep their word and fulfill all of their obligations. At the same time, they indicate the expectation that each individual member of the team will follow through on the obligations that are specifically assigned to them.

Greater comes from having less

We are referring to the manner in which we exhibit ourselves to others who are in our immediate environment when we use the phrase "lesser is greater." Keep in mind that the leader of the Ego Maniacs is so puffed up with pride that they steal all of the oxygen from the room. The concept that "lesser is greater" may be encapsulated in a single word: humility.

There are others who believe that humility and leadership are diametrically opposed qualities that have nothing in do with one another. I do not agree with you. Someone who is modest is someone who is easy to talk to. A person who is arrogant cannot be approached in any way.

It is essential for leaders to be approachable. They have the same humanity as the individuals they guide in their roles as leaders. Those who hold positions of leadership and are aware that they do not always have all the answers and that they do not claim to be flawless are being honest. They are demonstrating the virtue of real humility.

There is a happy medium to be found between arrogance and modesty. A leader has to have confidence, but they also need to learn how to be humble. The three terms—confidence, arrogance, and pride—are not interchangeable.

When a person feels proud of themselves, they are more likely to have an inflated view of themselves, sometimes known as a "egomaniac." Because of the narcissistic opinion they have of themselves, they might put themselves in harm's way unnecessarily.

A healthy type of self-esteem is confidence, which

may be defined as an accurate assessment of one's capabilities. It is possible to have both confidence and humility at the same time, yet egoism and humility are on completely different ends of the spectrum.

The quality of humility allows us to remain grounded and to examine our strengths and flaws, as well as the areas in which we may make improvements. Our arrogance prevents us from making sound judgments and compels us to disregard our shortcomings. Arrogant people almost never develop these flaws, which prevents them from making progress in their own personal development.

It is important to note that a modest leader is not synonymous with a weak leader. When circumstances present themselves that need a forceful reaction, it is important to behave in an authoritative manner. This in no way lessens the humility of the individual.

Great leaders are able to strike a balance between other beneficial attributes such as aggressiveness, humility, and confidence. It is not true that a modest person is incapable of advocating for oneself or taking the initiative just because they are humble.

The ability to demonstrate their humanity is made possible by humility in leaders. This garners respect from the individuals around them, and in certain instances, it even transfers to other people. This chapter may be summed up in one question, which is presented below. Consider the following scenario: there are two people standing in front of you, and you have the ability to choose one of them to serve as your direct supervisor.

You are familiar with both of them, and you are aware of their abilities as well as their personalities. Both candidates are equally qualified for the job, having received the same amount of schooling and having equivalent amounts of professional experience.

However, one of them has a personality that is characterized by extreme arrogance (The Ego Manaic), and the other is self-assured but also modest (The Respected Leader).

Who would you want to lead your team if you could choose anyone? If there were no other options, nobody would choose to be with the egomaniac rather than the other people. Now consider this: if you display qualities of an egomaniac, would people want to work with you as their boss if you exhibited such characteristics?

Unfortunately, we don't always get to pick who will be our boss; but, we do get to decide what kind of leadership approach we will follow.

Diversity And Equal Opportunity For Everyone

Within the context of today's globalized world...

The topic of work-life balance came up in our conversation as we walked down the beach this time, which was on a more personal level. Aaron was pleased to have Myra as his wife since he believes it enriches the cultural foundation of his family values. Your exposure to people and practices from a variety of cultures will help you develop a deeper understanding of the world. After a while, one thing led to another, and eventually the topic of discussion shifted to globalization and how it has brought people from all over the globe closer together.

In his explanation, Aaron said, "The famous book 'The world is flat' by Thomas L. Friedman reflects on how globalization has resulted in a smaller world." The rise of modern technology has, for the most part, eliminated barriers between different sectors of the economy, communities, cultures, and individuals all over the globe. The whole workforce has undergone a sea change as a result of globalization. The mixing of people from different civilizations and their own cultures results in a profound shift in viewpoint.

The most important thing to consider is whether or not variety stimulates innovation. Without a doubt, you are correct. The fact that individuals of different cultural backgrounds offer more inventive thoughts and the ability to find novel solutions to problems is the most compelling argument in favor of diversity. The obstacle that has to be overcome is effectively bringing together the workforce. Leaders are responsible for providing ongoing training for their staff on how to be aware of and sensitive to the multi-cultural, varied, and inclusive dynamics of the workforce.

Sleek was the term that was used to describe their outdoor kitchen area since it was simple but beautiful and in flow with the rest of the home. since they proceeded towards the outdoor kitchen area, the word "sleek" was used to describe their barbecue area. Myra's preparations for the lunch had already gotten under way. I welcomed her as we neared the kitchen, and she returned the greeting shortly after we entered.

When I offered my assistance, Aaron's response was, "Of course. In fact, why don't you and Myra discuss it while I cook? I have an important call to take." Harvey, I'll see you in a moment! Remember to make use of Myra's previous expertise working in the business sphere.

Myra is a top executive at a large company, and her approach to leadership is one that cannot be replicated by anybody else. She is able to provide you with a variety of viewpoints on the process of self-transformation. She is going to be really important in light of the fact that we just finished talking about globalization, diversity, and inclusion. He flashed a grin before leaving.

"Oh my God! That is really impressive. Your thoughts on any and all of these would be very much appreciated. Therefore, may I ask: do you also belong to The Q Club?

"No! putting in hard effort while patiently waiting for a chance to succeed at anything. Despite this, I am well aware of it due to the fact that I was the first one to profit from his time spent at The Q Club. It had a profound impact on both our professional and personal lives. In the future, I want to be able to take part in the spiritual and illustrative experience for myself. She exclaimed in an animated manner.

Her manner exudes a positive energy that is totally spiritual, proving that Aaron was correct in his assessment. I was blown away, and I responded by saying, "Even though Aaron made sure the experience is surreal, I agree with you one hundred percent on this." Since I first learned about the club, I've been counting down the days until I'm good enough to join the exclusive group of members. I was actually happy about it.

Aaron came back and joined us.

As we were getting ready for the brunch, I continued by asking, "As a leader, how do you think about diversity and inclusion, and why is it important in the workplace?"

Aaron smiled and responded while saying, "Myra is the best example here because she possesses both of the elements that we discussed." She is a lady who originates from a different nation and culture. I will hand this situation over to her and allow her to respond to the majority of your inquiries on this matter.

Myra beamed and said with a grin, "It's an honor to contribute. There is a considerable body of research that shows diversity has several benefits, including increased productivity and innovation, increased profitability, and an overall improvement in culture. In a working environment that is inclusive of all people, everyone receives fair treatment and has equal access to opportunities and resources. As a result, it is essential for a leader to comprehend this facet and put it into practice in order to ensure the success of the firm.

The genesis of the idea of inclusive leadership may be traced back to the phenomenon of globalization. A leadership that is inclusive demonstrates a capacity to comprehend and accommodate differences in its employees, customers, ideas, and employees' abilities. There is a long list of considerations that inclusive leaders need to bear in mind, including the following:

Leaders make the promotion of diversity and inclusion a top priority in their organizations.

provide Room: By keeping their own opinions to themselves, they provide room for others, making it easier for others to voice their opinions and share their perspectives.

Sensitivity: They encourage an open mind and sensitivity for the customs and traditions of other peoples.

They believe in adapting their customs to those of others and honoring the cultures of those with whom they interact.

Unity of the Team: Belief that varied cooperation is advantageous to the company is one factor that contributes to the empowerment of others and the cohesiveness of the team.

Aaron said, "Myra is one of the front runners promoting the global culture in our industry, and she is doing so by leading by example herself." Her conception of leadership carries a lot of weight. Her ethnic beliefs, mindfulness, and spirituality all come together to create a potent combination that gives her strength. This enables her to maintain composure and poise even under the most trying of circumstances.

Her leadership is distinguished by the fact that she encourages her team members to enjoy the holidays and traditions of a variety of countries. In addition to this, she is a speaker who often visits educational institutions such as colleges and schools to promote and raise awareness of diversity issues. It is hoped that by doing so, parents will be able to instill in their children an appreciation of many cultures, which will, in turn, make their children's lives more fulfilling and intriguing.

"Outstanding! " You are certainly a motivation for others!"

Myra showed her appreciation by nodding her head.

Having said that, I do have a question: "How is diversity different from inclusion?" It does sound slightly similar, doesn't it?"

Myra gave the following response: "Inclusion refers to the behaviors and social norms that ensure people feel welcomed, whereas diversity refers to the traits and characteristics that make people feel like they belong." Not only is inclusiveness essential to the success of diversity's efforts, but also the creation of an inclusive culture has been shown to be beneficial for employee engagement and productivity.

A point that has been noted, "Interesting perspective, so what are the various types of diversity that we are talking about?"

Myra responded by saying, "Diversity in the workplace is about more than gender, race, and ethnicity." It now has employees who come from a variety of backgrounds in terms of their religious and political beliefs, education, socioeconomic status, sexual orientation, cultural backgrounds, and even disabilities. Companies are learning that there are benefits that extend beyond what is visible on the surface when they actively support and promote an inclusive and diverse work environment.

However, since this is a field that is constantly being researched, we can talk about important diversities such as gender, age, ethnicity, social status, disabilities, and so on.

The following is a summary of the various types of diversity, according to the industry and the business world.

There Are A Lot Of Surprising Facts About Angela Merkel That You Probably Don't Know.

One may be surprised or perhaps astonished to learn that this German chancellor has held her position longer than any other woman in the country's history. These items are as follows:

1. Angela Merkel is the elected leader of Europe who has held her position for the greatest amount of time.

At the moment, Angela Merkel has the title of the longest-serving elected female leader in Europe; nevertheless, her tenure does not even come close to matching that of the monarchically-elected Queen Elizabeth II of the United Kingdom. In 2005, Merkel won the election to serve as Chancellor of

Germany, and she has held that position continuously since then.

2. Angela is an accomplished pastry chef and general kitchen hand.

Angela Merkel is the kind of person who enjoys bragging about her abilities in the kitchen and the bakery. In point of fact, her plum cake has garnered a lot of attention, and many people have complimented her cooking and baking skills. Potato soup and roulade are two of the dishes that she enjoys cooking the most. She was still able to find time to perform her cooking and baking at home while serving as a minister under Helmut Kohl. This was the case even though she was serving in that capacity.

3. Her paternal grandpa was of Polish descent.

Ludwig Kazmierczak is Angela Merkel's grandpa. He was born in Poland. In the year 1896, he was born in the city of Poznan, which was situated in Poland but was a part of Germany at the time. In the 1930s, her grandfather made the decision to alter the family name to Kasner, which is a German name. In the process of Germanizing the family name, the Kazmierczaks followed a conventional pattern.

4. "Mutti" is Angela's informal nickname.

The Germans have dubbed Angela Merkel "Mutti" due to the fact that she does not have any children of her own to call her own. Mutti is another word for mama. They chose this name for her in recognition of the sort of lady that she is. She is the kind of lady that puts everyone else's needs before her own, and she has a kind and generous heart.

Because she is a kind lady with a big heart, she was able to open her doors to immigrants seeking asylum in her nation.

5. She suffers from a crippling phobia of dogs.

Angela Merkel had a dog bite in the middle of the 1990s, which contributed to the development of her lifelong phobia of canines. At his vacation villa on the Black sea, Vladimir Putin let his formidable black Labrador, named Kony, to come inside. Because Merkel had a severe phobia of dogs, as soon as she noticed how menacing the dog was, she sat completely still and couldn't move.

6. Angela is the most powerful lady in the whole planet.

Many people believe that Angela Merkel is the most powerful woman to ever hold political office. As chancellor of Germany, she was able to achieve and complete more than in her previous role. In 2015, Forbes ranked Angela Merkel as the most powerful female leader in the world, placing her at the top spot on their list of the 100 most influential women in the world.

7. She has a native command of the Russian language.

Merkel was successful in acquiring the Russian language, and as a result, she was able to interact well with Vladamir Putin, who was a native Russian speaker.

8. She has a great deal of experience in the scientific field.

Marie Curie, who was the first woman to earn a Nobel Prize, served as an inspiration for her. Angela was the only woman working in the theoretical chemistry branch of the East German Academy of Science. She had degrees in quantum chemistry as well as physics, and she held the post there.

9. Angela has retained the surname of her first spouse.

The marriage between Angela and her first husband, Ulrich Merkel, who was a student of physics, lasted for just five years. Since 1998, she has been wed to Joachim Sauer, who comes from a prior marriage and is the father of their two kids. She still addresses her new spouse by her former husband's name, despite the fact that she is now married to another guy.

10. She is a seasoned performer who is adept at impressions

Angela Merkel enjoys impersonating the leaders of other countries in her spare time. These international leaders include Vladimir Putin, Pope Benedict XVI, the former President of France Nicolas Sarkozy, and even Al Gore, who served as the Vice President of the United States from 2000 to 2003. She is a capable leader who enjoys engaging in activities that leave a positive impression on the subjects she governs.

The Art Of Influencing Others

Leadership and influence are like two halves of a Siamese twin; they are inextricably linked, yet operate as independent spheres that are dependent on one another for survival. It is necessary to possess the trait of persuasion if one aspires to hold a position of leadership and influence others. The power to exert influence is a crucial component of effective leadership. To be a good leader, you need to be able to exert a lot of influence on other people. When a person's thoughts, emotions, or actions are changed as a result of the efforts of another person, we say that person has been effectively influenced. Influence may be found in all aspect of life, but it is most crucial for a leader since it is their primary tool for achieving success. The capacity to exert influence is one of the most essential skills for a leader to possess. To have any chance of persuading others to view things from his perspective, a person in a position of leadership has to have complete faith in the accomplishment of his own objectives and the viability of his own vision. A leader has the ability to influence people based on how passionately he can express his viewpoint. To successfully influence others, a leader has to possess high levels of both persuasion and self-assurance.

The level of someone's motivation is what makes them susceptible to being swayed either by the desire to get a reward or the desire to avoid receiving a punishment. Understanding the people he seeks to persuade is the first step a leader must take in order to choose the most effective means of persuasion to use. It is essential for a person in a position of leadership to set a good example for followers by acting in a way that reflects the values they espouse. Communication is a powerful tool that may be used to influence other individuals. Leaders have the ability to sway followers by painting a captivating picture of the future for their followers and motivating them to follow in the leader's footsteps.

By pointing others in the right direction to concentrate on, one may influence them to become more motivated to make the leader's vision a reality. They help people in ways that fulfill their dreams, give them a feeling of purpose, and leave them with a profound sense of satisfaction when the task is done. They strengthen and concentrate individuals in ways that fulfill their visions. Leaders inspire followers to adopt new ways of thinking and behaving by demonstrating such behaviors and by promoting fresh perspectives on existing circumstances. In doing so, they provide followers with the vocabulary and the fortitude necessary to articulate and implement these novel approaches. The leaders of today are educators, mentors, and role models who earn the bulk of their success via influence. These individuals are most likely to become successful.

In order for a leader to effectively influence others, he has to pay attention to every tiny detail that is involved in influencing others. This includes expressing interest in the people he is trying to influence, remembering their name regardless of how insignificant they may imagine they are, constantly listening to the people he is trying to influence, and making the people he is trying to influence feel important and loved. Smiling at someone constantly might give them the impression that you adore them and are on good terms with them, which may encourage them to support what you are trying to do. This brought back fond memories of my first day at an organization that I had joined while I was still in school. The president extended a personal invitation to me for lunch, which turned out to be my very first encounter in that capacity. Even when I moved away from the location where the association was situated, this one attitude on their part never convinced me to stop being a part of it.

Several Useful Pointers Regarding The Search For Inspiration

Being in a good mood is one easy thing you can do to assist yourself discover the inspiration you need. Make a radical shift in your mentality. In order to make this transformation, you will need to use reason and logic to fight against the harmful beliefs. Make an effort to think about the difficulties that you face rather than the traps that you face. You will have the opportunity to develop more and become more skilled in your area of specialization with each new issue.

As was previously indicated, recognizing even the most little of victories along the route may act as a continuous source of encouragement for the duration of your trip. This is not only an empty gesture of congratulation; rather, it is an acknowledgment of the fact that the accomplishment of every significant objective is the product of a series of smaller ones. Every single one of these moves brings you one step closer than you were before.

feel someone to support you if you feel that a significant part of your motivation in life comes from meeting the standards set by other people and then exceeding those standards. This may need you to share your objective with another person so that they may hold you responsible for achieving it. You may ask a buddy to check in on how things are going for you from time to time. You could also find that support groups provide a method for you to satisfy these requirements in the company of people who have the same aspirations. Every person will find a distinct set of answers to their problems, and it is up to you to discover how to kindle your own flame.

You may also need to figure out a means to keep your long-term aim in mind at all times. Keeping one's focus on the overarching goal may make even the most little and bothersome sacrifices more bearable. Your efforts will not go unrewarded in a short amount of time. Keep a careful eye on the process as it all comes together.

Last but not least, make a deal with yourself that you will only do it for the first thirty seconds in order to get started. When working toward a goal, the first step is often the one that presents the most challenge. Make a pact with yourself that you will only participate in the activity and stay going for a total of thirty seconds in order to break out of the rut of not taking any action. After then, you are free to leave at any time, although it is quite probable that you will choose to continue. It is far simpler to continue doing it than it is to start over again.

I believe that if you want to be a good leader, you should present yourself in a way that is consistent with that role. People are more likely to react positively to leaders who are clean, well-groomed, and dressed correctly. In his book "How to Get Rich," Donald Trump asserts that "the way we dress says a lot about us before we have ever spoken a word." I recommend that you make an investment in clothing of the highest possible quality that you are able to buy. The vast majority of managers do not understand the significance of this idea. Do not misunderstand me; I am not suggesting that you run out and spend a fortune on new clothing and accessories. It is not necessary to wear clothing from a well-known brand in order to have a good appearance. A decent watch can often be purchased for roughly fifty bucks. It won't cost you more than thirty bucks to get a decent pair of khakis. You need to maintain a nice appearance by keeping your fingernails trimmed and your hair cut short. When you walk into a room, people immediately take note of your looks. Simply putting effort into your appearance might make others see you as a more capable leader. It is important that you dress as though you do want to be noticed by other people. Being too flamboyant is never more appealing than displaying elegance. When they are at work, men in leadership roles shouldn't strive to look like rock stars. The women shouldn't try to look as fashionable as the next model to appear on television. At the workplace, you should avoid using an excessive amount of body spray or fragrance. There is a possibility that some individuals are allergic to the odor, while others may feel that it is distracting to their job. You will fare much better if you make an effort to wear just a trace quantity of a quality fragrance.

"Allow yourself some time to think things through, but when it's time to act, put your thoughts aside and get to work." President Andrew Jackson

15. Different Types of Leadership

Now we have arrived at the conclusion. Let's make an effort to piece everything together. It is my opinion that you will be a successful leader if you put the guidance included in this book to practice. Is there a single best approach to take charge? No. There is no one, flawless method of leading people that can be broken down into steps. There are leaders who guide others and there are leaders who encourage others. The instruction is clear and concise, and it explains to the employees what they are expected to perform. A warm and concerned attitude is indicative of a helpful boss. Combining the two approaches may be fruitful at times. The characteristics of the worker will determine which of these approaches will be most successful. As a leader, it is your responsibility to make up for the things that your worker lacks. A leader and a coach have very similar responsibilities. The coach of a football team does not actually toss the football;

instead, he communicates the play to the quarterback so that the quarterback may carry it out. Become a coach. Be the mentor that your workers are looking for and need from you. On other occasions, there is a single correct path. Being encouraging and helpful to a new employee who lacks previous experience is likely to provide greater results. If you have an experienced worker, you may find that being more straightforward is to your advantage. Take your time and be sure to have an open mind. No matter what kind of work you do, whether it be in the business sector or at the grocery store down the street, there is always something new to learn. Make the most of the opportunity, and don't forget to have fun. You should try to be of assistance to other people. According to John Gardner, once you begin to serve others, life loses its meaninglessness.

Conventions Governing Businesses Often Require Participation In Negotiations

During the time that I was attending school at an engineering school, I was witness to an event that was very fascinating. One of my male friends wanted me to set up a conversation between him and one of my female friends so that he could apologize to her for something that he had previously said to her. Despite the lack of clarity in my comprehension of the situation, I was willing to concede. At the cafeteria of our academic institution, I paid a visit to a female friend without first letting her know that I was accompanied by a male buddy. I convinced myself that I was engaged in the honorable work of minimizing the disparities that existed between two individuals (both of whom were my friends). When my buddy's girlfriend came in, we were having a cup of tea in the canteen together. I was there with my male friend. To my astonishment, she immediately began shouting aggressively at my male companion! I was taken aback when she reprimanded me and said that her faith in me had diminished as a result of that particular occurrence. She departed. After some time had passed, I found out that my male buddy had severely insulted her at an earlier point in time. I greatly regret the fact that I played the "go-between" position between the two parties without consulting my female friend first, and I apologized to her for doing so. I was also upset with my male buddy since he had kept the specific purpose of the meeting a secret from me. I told him to come clean.

An error in communication was made when I failed to inform my female buddy about my male friend and the context of the situation when we were meeting; in other words, the communication did not go in both directions.

From a psychological point of view: Communication refers to an encounter that is meaningful and is based on feedback. It is impossible to say that communication has taken place between two or more parties unless there has been a "exchange and acceptance" of the respective offers or declarations. The cognitive architecture of humans demonstrates that communications have been going around in order to clarify the inter-personal understanding, the understanding between person and organization, or the understanding between organization and organization. A definitive proclamation of the communication pretext should be made prior to the realization of the scheduled convention. When the conscious mind and the subconscious mind (which stores memories from the past) are not in sync with one another, conflict occurs, and the communication aim becomes hazy. And if this kind of misunderstanding is realized, then it will likely lead to disputes and confrontations, which will result in losses for companies.

LEARNING goal FOR BUSINESS: Whenever we organize a meeting for the purpose of negotiating or establishing consensus, the contextual backdrop should be very obvious among all participating members; otherwise, the interaction goal at the meeting will turn out poorly.

General Approaches To The Evaluation Of Individuals

Because we rely on one another for our own existence, we humans are born with an innate need to comprehend one another. We also have the innate capacity to speculate on the thoughts and emotions of other people by watching them, drawing on the lessons we've learned from our own lives, and trying to picture what it would be like to be in their shoes.

On the other hand, given that none of us are flawless, we often err when we attempt to analyze another person. We put our faith in the wrong person, we hire workers who are dishonest, we let criminals go free while we punish innocent people, we form biases, and we fail to comprehend the people we love.

In order to lead lives that are secure, peaceful, and fruitful, having access to trustworthy assessments of other people is essential; hence, it is essential to acquire the skills necessary to effectively evaluate persons.

Performing analyses on groups of people may be done in a few different ways. It often entails doing things like the following:

Notes and Remarks

When doing people analysis, having sharp observation skills is very necessary. In addition to paying attention, you need to recall the specifics and refrain from dismissing or changing what you observe in any way. Take note that

Hygiene, dress, accessories, possessions, and health state are all aspects of appearance.

Positioning, body symbols, facial emotions, eye movements, and head and eyelid movements are all examples of body language.

Voice, including tempo, volume, and tone

Words, including topics, words, and ways in which they are spoken and written

Communication includes a person's speaking manner, the frequency with which they start talks, and the length of time they continue dialogues.

Interactions include the number of friends a person has, the kind of friends they have, and how that person interacts with other people.

Favorites include things like music, cuisine, locations, and activities, among other things.

Procedures for Asking Questions

There are certain situations in which observations on their own are not sufficient to provide the information that you want. When a situation like this arises, you may reap the benefits of asking unique questions that shed light on the other person's personality. Think About It:

How they react to your inquiries (including their body language, voice, pace, and degree of comfort, among other things).

What kinds of responses they provide

The language that they use.

Different types of personalities

A lot of individuals have tried to divide people's personalities into several categories. You may get understanding about the many types of individuals you meet by familiarizing yourself with these typologies.

Pay attention to the characteristics of the individual, and try to identify a personality type that best fits them.

You should look up personality tests and then respond using the characteristics of your target.

Conduct research to learn more about a certain category of individuals (for example, narcissists, overachievers, sad people, etc.).

Examine the relevant demographics and statistical data.

The study of psychology

The field of study known as psychology examines both the mind and behavior. If you want to be skilled at assessing others, including yourself, learning this topic is one of the greatest things you can learn to acquire. This topic covers a wide range of topics, including many different aspects of people's personalities, as well as their motivations and their communication styles. The more information you have, the better you will be able to comprehend another person.

Use as many of the aforementioned approaches as you can if you want your analysis to be as accurate as possible. If you want to prevent making errors, the principles that are presented in the previous chapter should be followed.

Keep in mind that everything about a person that you can see indicates something about that individual, but you shouldn't fix your judgments in stone unless you find substantial evidence to support them.

A person who dresses terribly, for instance, may have low self-esteem because they may believe they are not deserving of other people's attention. This is an easy assumption to make. Nevertheless, there are a few more hypotheses that might explain this:

He or she is self-assured to the point that they do not care what other people think.

Because they were running late, he or she did not have time to put together a nice outfit.

Because of how furious they are, they do not care about how they appear at all.

By doing further research, conducting interviews, and conducting observations, you will be able to determine which one is which.

The following chapter will cover non-verbal language, which is a rich source of information that may be obtained about a person in a very short amount of time.

www.ingramcontent.com/pod-product-compliance
Lightning Source LLC
Chambersburg PA
CBHW050359120526
44590CB00015B/1749